GREAT EXPEDITIONS

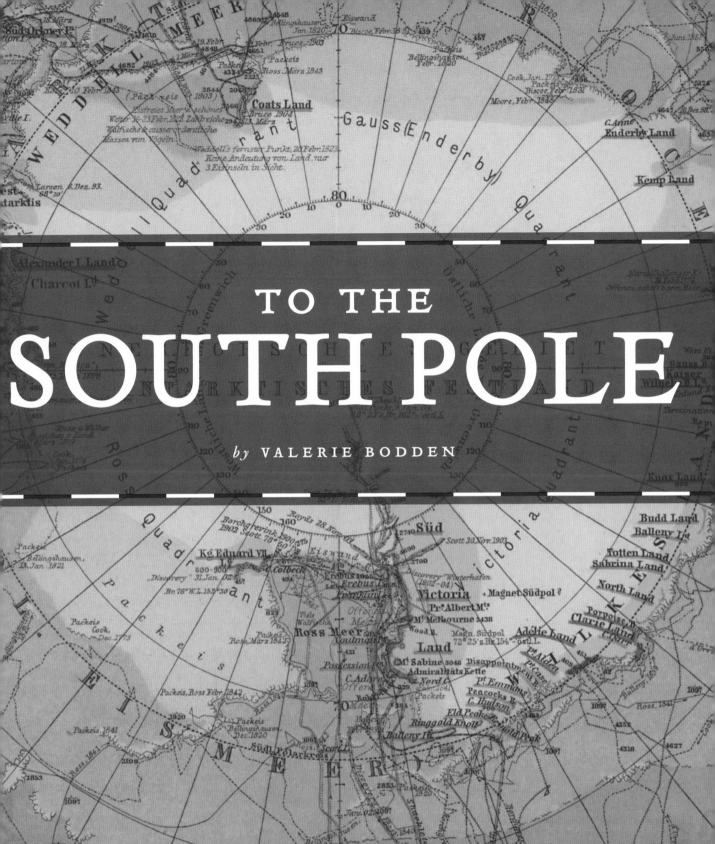

TO THE
SOUTH POLE

by VALERIE BODDEN

CREATIVE ◐ EDUCATION

PUBLISHED BY Creative Education
P.O. Box 227, Mankato, Minnesota 56002
Creative Education is an imprint of The Creative Company
www.thecreativecompany.us

DESIGN AND PRODUCTION BY Ellen Huber
ART DIRECTION BY Rita Marshall
PRINTED BY Corporate Graphics
in the United States of America

PHOTOGRAPHS BY
Alamy (Lordprice Collection, Photos 12, Photoshot Holdings Ltd),
Corbis (Bettmann, PoodlesRock), Dreamstime (Bernard Breton),
Getty Images (After William Henry Browne, David Boyer/National Geographic,
Hulton Archive, Mansell/Time & Life Pictures, Herbert Ponting/Scott
Polar Research Institute, University of Cambridge, Bob Thomas/Popperfoto,
Topical Press Agency), The Granger Collection, NYC, History-map.com,
iStockphoto (Nicholas Belton, Mike Bentley, Brandon Laufenberg), National Geographic
Stock (Norbert Wu/Minden Pictures), National Library of Australia

LIBRARY OF CONGRESS CATALOGING-IN-PUBLICATION DATA
Bodden, Valerie.
To the South Pole / by Valerie Bodden.
p. cm. — (Great expeditions)
Includes bibliographical references and index.
Summary: A history of Roald Amundsen's successful 1911 trip to the South Pole,
detailing the challenges encountered, the individuals involved, the discoveries made,
and how the expedition left its mark upon the world.

ISBN 978-1-60818-069-1
1. Amundsen, Roald, 1872–1928—Juvenile literature. 2. Explorers—Norway—
Biography—Juvenile literature. 3. South Pole—Discovery and exploration—Juvenile
literature. I. Title. II. Series.

G585.A6B57 2011
919.8'9—dc22 2010033552
CPSIA: 110310 PO1383

First Edition
2 4 6 8 9 7 5 3 1

TABLE OF CONTENTS

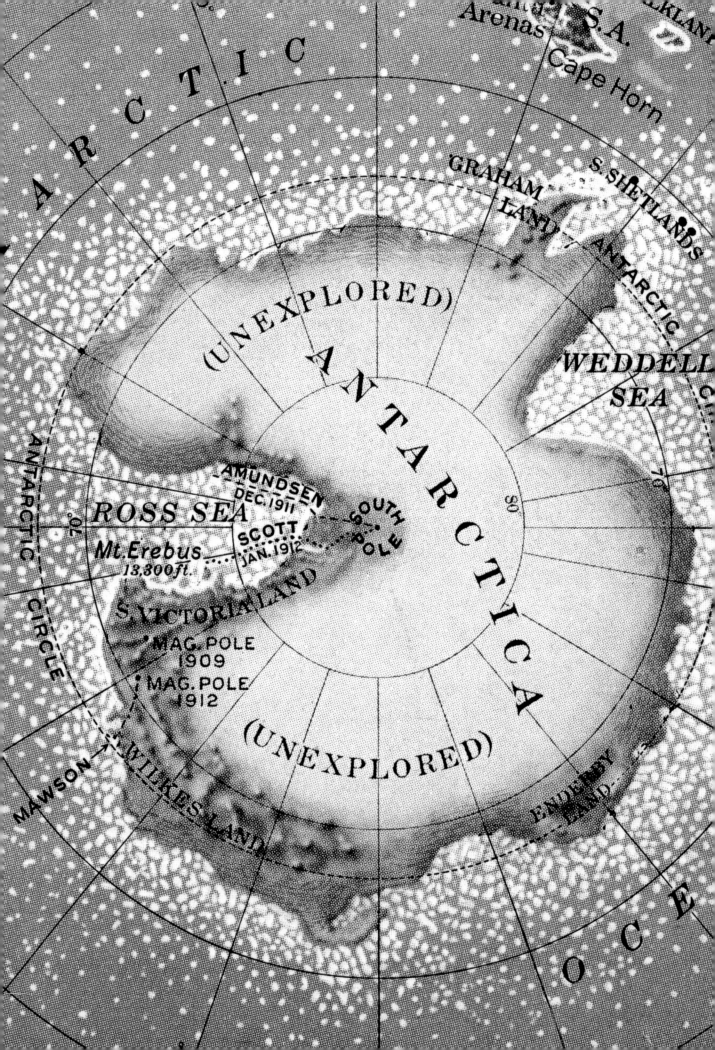

TERRA AUSTRALIS INCOGNITA

BY THE BEGINNING OF THE 20TH CENTURY, FEW "FIRSTS" REMAINED TO BE ACHIEVED IN THE FIELD OF GLOBAL EXPLORATION. THE COASTLINES OF NEARLY EVERY CONTINENT HAD BEEN CAREFULLY CHARTED, AND THEIR INTERIORS HAD BEEN OPENED BY ENTERPRISING EXPLORERS IN SEARCH OF WEALTH, MISSION FIELDS, OR JUST PLAIN ADVENTURE. YET

two areas of the world remained imperfectly documented: the poles. During the early 1900s, a fierce competition erupted as adventurers from around the world vied to be the first to reach the farthest points on the globe. In 1909, Americans Frederick Cook and Robert Peary emerged from the Arctic, claiming to have reached the North Pole on separate expeditions. Their announcements upset the preparations of another North-Pole-seeker, a Norwegian named Roald Amundsen, who quickly changed his plans and headed south. The decision was historic: in December 1911, he led the first successful expedition to the South Pole. The world's last unknown area of land had finally been reached.

The legendary expeditions of Roald Amundsen and Robert Scott are marked on this 1925 map of what was then a still unexplored Antarctica.

Long before Amundsen reached the South Pole, scientists and philosophers of the ancient world guessed at the existence of a great southern landmass, though no one would sail far enough south to confirm their suspicions for more than 2,000 years. During the 400s B.C., the Greek philosopher Parmenides theorized that the world could be divided into five climate zones and that the zones farthest north and south would be characterized by frigid temperatures. A century later, the Greek explorer Pytheas traveled as far north as the ARCTIC CIRCLE, where he encountered the northern PACK ICE.

Around the same time, the Greek philosopher

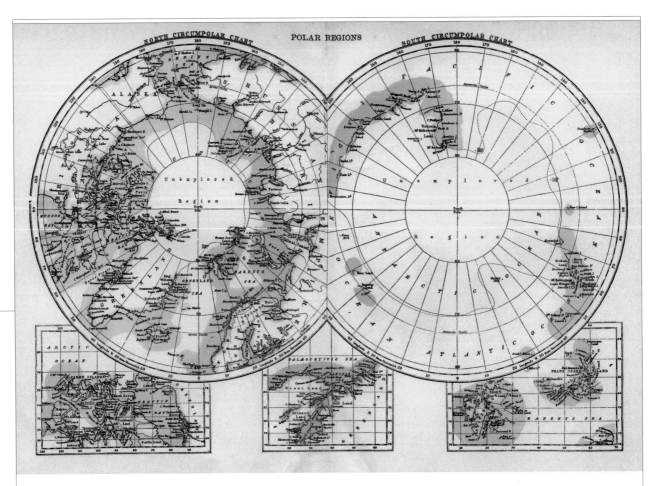

By the late 1800s, a rough outline of the Antarctic continent could be sketched on maps, but no one had as yet explored past the coastlines.

Aristotle, who subscribed to Parmenides' theory about climate zones, proposed that the landmass in the northern part of the world was balanced by land in the south. Because the constellation Arctos (the Greek term for Ursa Major, or the Great Bear constellation) could be seen in the northern sky, Aristotle gave the southern land the name Anti-Arctos, meaning "opposite to the north." Later maps labeled this land *Terra Australis Incognita*, or "The Unknown Southern Land." In the second century A.D., the Egyptian geographer Ptolemy speculated that this unknown land linked the known continents of Europe, Asia, and Africa. He also thought people lived and could grow food there. Three centuries after Ptolemy, Roman philosopher Ambrosius Macrobius drew the outline

EXPEDITION JOURNAL

Olav Bjaaland
January 11, 1911

At long last, the ice barrier [Ross Ice Shelf] hove [rose] into sight today. It is a strange feeling that grips one as the sight now reveals itself. The sea is still as a pond, and before one stands this Great Wall of China and glitters. Far off, it is like a photograph that has just been developed on the plate. By letting one's thoughts wander over the surface, one finds oneself in a melancholy mood. One thinks of what is to come, the hardships one is going to meet, the use one will be, and if we can get there before the Englishmen— who are surely burning with the same ambition.

of Terra Australis on a world map, despite the fact that its existence still hadn't been proven.

It wasn't until the great voyages of discovery in the 1400s and 1500s that Terra Australis began to take on a definite shape. After Portuguese explorer Ferdinand Magellan's ships circumnavigated (sailed all the way around) the globe from 1519 to 1522, proving definitively that the Earth was round, maps began to show a large, separate southern continent, extending as far north as the southern tips of South America, Africa, and Australia. As explorers sailed farther south during the next two centuries without discovering any signs of a large landmass, the hypothetical continent became smaller on maps until it was pictured within the confines of the ANTARCTIC CIRCLE.

Weddell seals, named for and discovered by British sealer James Weddell in the 1820s, are abundant in the icy waters surrounding Antarctica.

In 1768, British naval officer James Cook became the first to set out on an expedition dedicated to proving (or disproving) the existence of a southern continent. Although he did not come within sight of Antarctica on this voyage, Cook again sailed south in 1772. This time, he crossed the Antarctic Circle and continued south until he arrived at LATITUDE 71°10′ S, setting a new record for the farthest point south ever reached (the South Pole lies at latitude 90° S). At this latitude, Cook encountered pack ice and was unable to continue, so he circumnavigated Antarctica but saw only ice and small islands. When Cook returned to Great Britain in 1775, his reports of abundant seals in the Antarctic waters led American and British sealers to set sail for the south. Throughout the early 19th century, many of these sealers discovered new islands just outside the Antarctic Circle.

Then, in 1820, the Antarctic mainland was at last spotted, though who was actually the first to see it remains a matter of dispute, as explorers from Britain, the United States, and Russia all claimed that distinction. Two decades later, British naval officer James Clark Ross sailed through the Antarctic ICE BELT to latitude 78°10′ S in the sea that now bears his name. His progress southward was there stopped by a sheer ice cliff towering 160 to 200 feet (49–61 m) above the sea. After sailing nearly 450 miles (724 km) along the ICE SHELF and finding no opening, Ross named it the Great Ice Barrier (and it is now known as the Ross Ice Shelf).

The formidable Ross Ice Shelf extends for nearly 373 miles (600 km) and rises between 49 and 164 feet (15–50 m) above the water's surface.

During the half-century after Ross's discovery of the ice shelf, exploration of Antarctica tapered off, but in 1895, the sixth International Geographical Congress in London urged further exploration of the continent, ushering in what became known as the "Heroic Era" of Antarctic exploration. This was a time marked by fierce competition to reach the farthest point south—and, ultimately, the pole. In 1897, a Belgian expedition aboard the ship *Belgica* went in search of the southern magnetic pole (the area in the Southern Hemisphere where Earth's MAGNETIC FIELD is most intense). Among the ship's crew was Roald Amundsen, serving as first mate. During the voyage, the *Belgica* became trapped in the pack ice, and its crew, though ill-prepared, became the first to spend the winter in the Antarctic.

During the first decade of the 20th century, expeditions from Germany, Sweden, Britain, and France traveled to Antarctica, charting the coastline and carrying out scientific observations. In

Ernest Shackleton first made history (along with Edward Wilson and Robert Scott, above) when the landmark of 82°17' S was reached on December 31, 1902.

1901, the first expedition to attempt to reach the South Pole embarked from Britain and was led by Robert Falcon Scott. The expedition fell far short of its goal, although it did reach a new "farthest south" record of 82°17' S in December 1902. The next attempt to reach the South Pole was led by British explorer Ernest Shackleton, who reached another record latitude of 88°23' S in 1909. At this point, he was only 97 miles (156 km) from the pole, but a dangerously low food supply forced him to turn back.

Only months after Shackleton's achievement, Scott was again planning an attempt on the South Pole. But he wasn't alone. Although no one knew it yet, Roald Amundsen was about to turn the trek to the South Pole into a race.

FRAM CREW PROFILE:
ROALD AMUNDSEN

Born on July 16, 1872, near Oslo, Norway, Roald Amundsen

decided at an early age to become an Arctic explorer.

Although he studied medicine to please his mother, after

her death in 1893, Amundsen left school and took part in

both Arctic and Antarctic expeditions before setting out

for the South Pole in 1910. From 1918 to 1922, Amundsen

led an unsuccessful attempt to reach the North Pole in the

ship *Maud*, and in 1926, he spearheaded an expedition that

flew over the North Pole in the AIRSHIP *Norge*, becoming,

with Oscar Wisting, the first people to reach both poles. In

1928, Amundsen set out to rescue the *Norge*'s pilot, Umberto

Nobile, after his new airship, *Italia*, crashed in the Arctic.

Amundsen's plane took off on June 18, 1928, but he was

never seen again.

Last of the Vikings

Born near Oslo, Norway, less than 450 miles (724 km) from the Arctic Circle, Roald Amundsen decided at the age of 15 to become an Arctic explorer. He was inspired by the writings of British explorer Sir John Franklin, who had died in 1847 while attempting to locate the Northwest Passage, the long-rumored water route through the North American continent. In preparation for a life of Arctic exploration, Amundsen played football to condition his body, skied the mountains around Oslo to improve his skill in traversing over snow and ice, and even slept with his bedroom window open during the winter to become immune to the Arctic cold. Such behaviors earned him the nickname "the last of the Vikings."

Amundsen's first experience of the Arctic was as a sailor on the seal-hunting vessel *Magdalena* from 1894 to 1896. Afterward, he joined the *Belgica* expedition to Antarctica, assuming command of the ship after the captain fell ill with scurvy. During the course of the journey, Amundsen proved his worth as a polar explorer, instructing that warm suits be made out of the ship's blankets and that the men eat fresh seal meat to ward off scurvy.

By the time he returned from Antarctica, Amundsen was ready to lead his own expedition, and in 1903, he set out on the *Gjøa* on his own attempt to navigate the Northwest Passage. Three years later, he returned to Norway successful, having been the first to sail through the passage and around the northern Canadian coast. Amundsen's next goal was to reach the North Pole. In September 1909, he was in the midst of preparing for a polar expedition when he received news that

Even amidst the desolate landscape of Antarctica, Roald Amundsen perhaps felt at home, traveling on skis as he had in his native Norway.

The Fram *had been used by Amundsen's hero Fridtjof Nansen during his Arctic voyage of 1893–96.*

Cook and Peary had already arrived. Days later, Amundsen decided his expedition would go to the South Pole instead.

Although Amundsen had made his decision, he did not tell anyone of it, aside from his brother (who was his business manager) and the captain of his vessel, the *Fram* (Norwegian for "forward"). He feared that if news of his plans became public, his financial backers might withdraw their support. He also worried that Scott, an officer in the powerful British navy, might try to prevent him from basing his expedition in the Ross Sea, which Scott had come to regard as his own personal exploration headquarters.

With money provided by government grants and private investors (as well as credit taken out on personal accounts), Amundsen began to outfit his 18-man crew. In a land where temperatures rarely rise above 0 °F (-17.8 °C)—and often sink well below—warm clothing would be essential in preventing hypothermia (a condition characterized by dangerously low body temperature), frostbite, and ice burns.

EXPEDITION JOURNAL

ROALD AMUNDSEN
May 22, 1911

ood weather. Still and clear -46°.... Tomorrow we will have the door to the entrance installed, and thereby the whole of this huge snow complex will be finished.... It is difficult to describe the beautiful scene I saw when I came out of my dog tent this afternoon. Low down on the S.W. horizon was the moon—shining yellow—just over the rooftop of our hut—or snow mound. In the S.W. sky the Southern Lights played in many forms and colors—and high up there one sees the Southern Cross [constellation] among an army of glittering, shining worlds. Like a fairy tale, the big, pointed ... tents rise up, all illuminated as if in celebration.... If only I could paint—if only I could.

Amundsen purchased thick, woolen undergarments, wool sweaters, sealskin suits, windproof oversuits, and reindeer-skin jackets and pants for himself and those crew members who would join him on the trek through Antarctica. Food provisions included chocolate, powdered milk, biscuits, jam, fruit, cheese, tea, sugar, and coffee. High-energy pemmican cakes—mixtures of dried meat, melted fat, vegetables, and oatmeal—were also brought for the long overland journey.

Once valued by explorers, sled dogs have been banned from Antarctica since 1993 because of a disease they spread to seals.

Amundsen planned to spend the winter in Antarctica preparing for the attempt on the South Pole and had the parts for a wooden hut—to serve as a shelter—constructed. He also ordered tools, such as saws and ice drills, and scientific and navigational instruments, including SEXTANTS, compasses, thermometers, barometers, and HYPSOMETERS. Snowshoes and skis would help the men cross Antarctica's ice and snow.

Among Amundsen's most important purchases were nearly 100 Greenland huskies. He had become convinced of the value of sled dogs during his previous trips to the Arctic. Dogs could provide warning of deep, wide cracks in the ice known as crevasses; if they fell in, the rest of the team would be alerted to the danger—and the dogs could safely be pulled out by their harnesses. In addition, dogs could be slaughtered along the way and fed to other dogs, thus reducing the amount of dog food that would need to be carried along.

By May 1910, Amundsen was ready to load his supplies onto the *Fram*, which had been built specifically for polar voyages, with a strong, rounded hull (main body) that could withstand the pressures of being frozen into pack ice. In June, the crew boarded the ship and

set sail on a month-long test voyage in the Atlantic. By the end of July, the *Fram* had returned to Norway to pick up additional supplies, including the dogs, and embark for its true destination—which most of the crew still believed to be the North Pole.

On August 9, 1910, the *Fram* pulled out of the harbor and set course for Madeira, an island near Portugal. Since the plan for the voyage to the North Pole was to sail around South America and then go north toward the Arctic Ocean, the men aboard were not suspicious when the *Fram* first headed south. From Madeira, however, they would now have to sail around the southern tip of Africa instead of South America, so it was here that Amundsen informed his crew of their true destination. Despite the change in plans, all were eager to continue. As he left Madeira, Amundsen sent a telegram to Scott, informing the British explorer that he, too, was planning to travel to the South Pole.

By October 4, the *Fram* had reached the equator, having covered about 5,000 miles (8,047 km) of its 16,000-mile (25,750 km) sea voyage. Soon, it was sailing south of Africa, where the crew had to begin watching for icebergs. The first was spotted on New Year's Day 1911, and the next day, the ship crossed into the Antarctic Circle. Now, in the heart of the southern summer (which occurs at the same time as winter in the Northern Hemisphere), the sun remained above the horizon 24 hours a day, and the *Fram* maneuvered into the ice belt, where it was surrounded by large sheets of ice on all sides. Four days later, it was through the ice and into the swells of the Ross Sea. After sailing another 500 miles (805 km), the *Fram* arrived at the Bay of Whales, a natural harbor along the Ross Ice Shelf, on January 14, 1911, and was moored along the sea ice.

FRAM CREW PROFILE:
OLAV BJAALAND

Olav Bjaaland was born on March 5, 1873, in Morgedal,
Norway. One of the best skiers of his day, Bjaaland won the
Nordic combined event (a combination of ski jumping and
cross-country skiing) at the Holmenkollen Ski Festival in
1902, and in 1908, he came in second in the 30-mile (50 km)
race. The next year, he met Amundsen, who invited him
to join the expedition to what they then thought would be
the North Pole. During the expedition, Bjaaland showed
his skill as a carpenter, rebuilding the team's sleds to save
weight. In the years following the expedition, Bjaaland set
up a ski factory with money lent to him by Amundsen. In
1952, Bjaaland was chosen to light the Olympic torch in his
hometown of Morgedal for the Oslo Winter Olympics. He
died in 1961.

Antarctic blizzards are known for their ferocity; Australian Douglas Mawson (pictured) documented blizzards with wind speeds greater than 60 miles (97 km) per hour.

To the Pole

*D*URING THE VOYAGE SOUTH, AMUNDSEN HAD CHOSEN EIGHT MEN— HELMER HANSSEN, OSCAR WISTING, SVERRE HASSEL, OLAV BJAALAND, JØRGEN STUBBERUD, ADOLF LINDSTRØM, KRISTIAN PRESTRUD, AND HJALMAR JOHANSEN—TO REMAIN WITH HIM ON LAND. NOW THESE MEN, WHO WOULD BE STRANDED ON THE ICE SHELF WHILE THE REST OF THE

crew made scientific observations in the South Atlantic aboard the *Fram*, set out to establish a winter camp. About 4 miles (6.4 km) from the sea—and 870 miles (1,400 km) from the South Pole—they erected their hut, which they named Framheim (meaning "home of *Fram*"). Working in summertime temperatures ranging from only -13 to 5 °F (-25 to -15 °C), the men soon had Framheim completed, and they moved in on January 28.

The party then began to prepare for the coming winter by stocking up on fresh meat. Weddell and crabeater seals were abundant in the area and, since they had no natural predators on land, were easy targets. By the end of

Amundsen used measurements of the sun's position above the horizon to get his bearings when traveling on land during polar expeditions.

summer, the men had stored 60 tons (54 t) of seal meat. Although there were not many penguins in the Bay of Whales, those that were seen also became meals, as did large birds called great skuas.

With winter preparations well underway, Amundsen turned his thoughts toward the race ahead. His goal of reaching the South Pole before Scott hinged on a plan of stashing food supplies in key locations along the route so that the dogs would not have to transport supplies dedicated for the return journey all the way to the pole. From February to April, the men established three such supply caches, at latitudes 80°, 81°, and 82° S. Altogether, they stored three

Whether at points north (above) or south, Amundsen believed that transportation by dog sled was the most effective and efficient mode.

tons (2.7 t) of provisions—including seal meat, pemmican, and kerosene, an oil used for powering portable stoves.

Winter had set in by the time they finished, and the sun sank below the horizon on April 19, not to be seen again for four months. The men dug tunnels and rooms for workshops deep into the ice, connecting them to their hut—which was itself buried in snow—so that there would be little need to go outside, where temperatures regularly plunged below -58 °F (-50 °C). Then they set to work preparing their gear for the journey to the South Pole by lightening the wooden sleds, sewing new, lightweight underclothing, and pulling their boots apart and stitching them back together to make them larger.

By the end of August, the sun had reappeared, and the sleds were packed. On September 8, the men set out for the pole, only to be driven back by temperatures of -60 °F (-51 °C) and below, which killed several dogs and left the men with frostbite. After returning to Framheim, Amundsen divided the team into two parties. One would attempt the South Pole, and the other would explore King Edward VII Land (today's King Edward Peninsula) to the east. He thought that a smaller party would be able to reach the pole faster and with fewer supplies.

EXPEDITION JOURNAL

ROALD AMUNDSEN
December 1, 1911

How often have I not discovered that a day one expects nothing of—brings much. A south easterly blizzard ... overnight had half persuaded me to declare a rest day for the dogs. But, during a little lull, we agreed to try and travel. It was cold to begin with. During the night the wind had swept large areas of the glacier bare and free of snow. The crevasses were horrible.... But we managed inch by inch, foot by foot, sledge [sled] length by sledge length, sometimes east, sometimes west, sometimes north, sometimes south, round huge open chasms and treacherous crevasses about to collapse.... But we managed and, after a time [traveling in] fog, gale and drift [we found] the chasms more and more filled with snow ... until we reached the plateau, where they completely ceased.

Finally, on October 19, the weather had warmed enough for the polar party—Amundsen, Hanssen, Wisting, Hassel, and Bjaaland—to set out with 4 sleds and 52 dogs. Heading first for their caches, the men quickly fell into a routine. Either Amundsen or Hassel would break the trail on skis, followed by the others driving the sled dogs. Along the way, they would erect six-foot-high (1.8 m) towers out of snow blocks to mark the route. When they stopped for the day, they would set up their tent and eat a meal of vegetable soup, pemmican, biscuits, and water.

Crevasses were dangerous obstacles for both men and dogs, and rescuing a person could be a harrowing and difficult task for his crewmen.

Although the way to the caches had been marked by flags, blizzards at first obscured the route, and the men stumbled onto a part of the ice shelf crisscrossed by crevasses. Although dogs occasionally fell into the seemingly bottomless cracks, the men were able to pull them out, and by November 1, they had passed the last of the crevasses. With the nearly flat ice shelf ahead of them, the men all strapped on their skis and let the dogs pull them along.

On November 6, the men left the last cache, at latitude 82° S, and moved into completely unknown territory. With no landmarks in sight, they relied on their compasses to navigate a course due south, while a "sledmeter" (a device consisting of a bicycle wheel attached to the back of each sled, with a meter that counted its revolutions) kept track of the distance traveled. Covering 23 miles (37 km) a day, the men reached a new degree of latitude about every 3 days, and at each degree, they established a cache. On November 17, they came to the end of the Ross Ice Shelf and the foot of a mountain chain, which they named the Queen Maud Mountains, after the queen of Norway.

As the party began to climb the mountains, they were confronted with a GLACIER that they named after Axel Heiberg, one of their Norwegian supporters. On the glacier, the intensity of the sunlight reflecting off the snow prompted the men to peel off their heavy outer clothing, and enormous blocks of ice and huge crevasses frequently forced them to backtrack and find another route. Finally, on November 20, they emerged onto the 10,920-foot-high (3,328 m) polar plateau, a high, flat plain of snow and ice. Here they set up camp and killed 24 dogs to provide fresh meat for the others (and themselves). Dividing the remaining dogs among three sleds (the fourth was left behind), the men set out again, struggling to draw a deep breath in the thin air of the plateau's higher altitude. They were soon confronted by another glacier, which they called Devil's Glacier. Despite blinding snowstorms, the party continued across the deeply crevassed surface.

On December 4, the men reached the edge of Devil's Glacier, and the ground evened out, allowing them to travel at a rapid pace, even in the midst of another blinding gale. The next day, however, their progress was slowed by hard, icy ridges in the snow known as sastrugi. On December 7, in improved ground and weather conditions, the men triumphantly raised a Norwegian flag on the lead sled as they passed 88°23′ S, the southernmost record set by Shackleton. They were now fewer than 100 miles (161 km) from their goal.

FRAM CREW PROFILE:
OSCAR WISTING

Born in Larvik, Norway, on June 6, 1871, Oscar Wisting
went to sea at the age of 16. From 1903 to 1906, he sailed
aboard a whaler near Iceland, and he was serving in the
Norwegian navy when Amundsen asked him to join the
Fram expedition. After returning from the South Pole,
Wisting joined Amundsen as first mate on an expedition
to reach the North Pole in the ship *Maud*. In 1926, Wisting
took part in Amundsen's flight over the Arctic in the
airship *Norge*. Two years later, when Amundsen's plane
disappeared, Wisting joined the search mission. Afterward,
he led efforts to build the Fram Museum in Oslo to display
the historic ship. On December 5, 1936, Wisting's body was
found in his old cabin aboard the *Fram*. He had died of a
heart attack.

THE RACE IS WON

As Amundsen and his men continued south past 88°23′ S, they crossed easily over the fluffy snow. On the afternoon of December 14, they stopped; the meters on their sleds indicated that they had traveled the full distance to the South Pole, 870 miles (1,400 km) from Framheim. There was no indication that anyone else had ever reached the spot—the race was won! Together, the five men planted the Norwegian flag in the snow, naming the vast plain on which they stood King Haakon VII's Plateau, after their king.

After getting a little rest, at 2:30 A.M., Bjaaland, Wisting, and Hassel traveled 12.5 miles (20 km) from the camp to the east, west, and south, so that, if they weren't already on the exact location of the pole, they would be sure to cover it in the course of their trek. Hanssen and Amundsen spent the day taking observations in order to determine their exact latitude. They found that they had reached 89°54′30″ S, 5.5 miles (8.9 km) north of the true pole. On December

Oscar Wisting (pictured) had the honor of planting the flag in the ice at the South Pole, along with Amundsen and the three other members.

16, the party journeyed these last 5.5 miles (8.9 km), then they took hourly observations for 24 hours, confirming with their instruments that they were as close to the South Pole as was possible. The men set up a tent (which they named Polheim), flying the Norwegian flag and the pennant of the *Fram*. In the tent they placed a record of their observations, a tablet listing their names, and a letter for Scott (who they expected would arrive soon) to carry to the Norwegian king, should anything happen to them on the return journey.

The party set out for Framheim on December 17, with a skiing Bjaaland in the lead. Before they left, Amundsen wrote in his diary, "And so farewell,

When the land party first crossed Devil's Glacier, the men had to carefully guide their sleds across many deep crevasses.

dear Pole. I don't think we'll meet again." By January 1, the party had arrived at Devil's Glacier, which they were able to cross this time in an area relatively free of crevasses. Descending the Axel Heiberg Glacier also proved to be an easy trip, lasting only hours rather than the several days it had taken to climb it, and by January 6, the men were once again on the Ross Ice Shelf. Thankful for the lower altitude, which allowed them to breathe more freely, the party traveled quickly—sometimes during the day and sometimes at night, as it was now light all the time—covering 20 or 30 miles (32–48 km) a day. As they traveled, they stopped at their caches to pick up supplies; they had stored so much extra food that they began to eat as much as they could to lighten their load, and both men and dogs began to put on weight. Early on the morning of January 25, just over three months after they had set out, the men were once again standing inside their hut at Framheim.

EXPEDITION JOURNAL

HELMER HANSSEN
of the arrival at the South Pole on December 14, 1911

[It was] a solemn moment for us all. As always, Amundsen thought of his companions, and when we planted the Norwegian flag at the South Pole, he let us all hold the bamboo stick with the flag, when it was fixed in the snow.... For my part, I had no feeling of triumph at that moment— as perhaps might have been expected. I was relieved to know that no longer would I have to stare down at the compass in the biting wind, which continually blew against us while we drove southwards, but which we now would have behind us.

Rejoining their four companions, who had returned as the first men to set foot on King Edward VII Land, Amundsen and the southern party learned that the *Fram* had already arrived. By January 30, the land party was back aboard the ship, and the *Fram* sailed out of the Bay of Whales. In early March, the crew reached Hobart, Tasmania, near Australia, and Amundsen telegraphed news of his success to King Haakon, as well as to *The Daily Chronicle* of London. People around the globe hailed the triumph, and *The New York Times* proclaimed, "The whole world has now been discovered."

Scott (in October 1911) was confident that his expedition was "as near perfection as experience can direct," yet his was an ill-fated journey.

When they returned to Europe, Amundsen and his party were greeted with adulation. Many British citizens were in mourning, though. Not only had Scott not been the first to reach the pole, but members of Scott's party had returned from Antarctica in February 1913 without their leader or the four men who had attempted the pole with him. Although the men had reached the South Pole on January 18, 1911 (just over a month after the Norwegians), they had died of starvation and exhaustion on their return journey. Scott's failure was largely a result of poor planning. He had not used dogs, established enough caches, or accounted for the men having to pull their heavily laden sleds for most of the journey after shooting their Siberian ponies, which proved useless in the deep snow. Scott's reputation as an eminent polar explorer remained intact for many years after his death, though, his status actually eclipsing Amundsen's, whose careful forethought had allowed his expedition to both reach the pole and return home safely.

Although saddened by Scott's unfortunate death—as well as by the perceived insignificance of his accomplishment, in comparison—Amundsen was soon planning his next expedition, which would take him back to the Arctic. In fact, Amundsen dedicated the rest of his life to Arctic exploration. A few former expedition members joined him in his new ventures.

Amundsen never returned to the Antarctic, but explorers from Japan, Australia, Germany, Britain, and other nations led expeditions there in later years. By the 1920s, seven countries had laid claim to land on the continent. During the International Geophysical Year (IGY) of 1957–58, scientists around the world researched the physical processes of Earth, the atmosphere, and the sun. At that time, worldwide attention was especially focused on Antarctica, and 12 nations—among them Argentina, the U.S., Australia, Britain, and Norway—established research stations there. Following the IGY, those 12 countries signed the

Scientists at Antarctic research stations study the environment around them, including such native wildlife as emperor penguins.

Fram Crew Profile:
Helmer Hanssen

Helmer Hanssen was born in 1870 in the village of
Risøyhamn, located on one of Norway's Vesterålen Islands,
which border the Arctic. In 1894, he began a career whaling
and sealing, and, in 1903, he joined Amundsen's expedition
through the Northwest Passage, during which he learned
dog driving from the native Inuit people. Hanssen's expertise
in handling sled dogs prompted Amundsen to invite him
to the South Pole. After returning from the pole, Hanssen
joined Amundsen as captain of the North-Pole-bound *Maud*.
Afterward, he worked in the Norwegian customs agency,
and in 1924, he joined a British expedition to study the
animal life and habitats of Spitsbergen, a Norwegian island
in the Arctic Ocean. Hanssen later worked as a ship inspector
and died in Tromsø, Norway, in 1956.

Antarctic Treaty, which declares that the continent belongs to no nation and that it "shall continue forever to be used exclusively for peaceful purposes." As of 2010, 47 countries had signed the treaty.

Today, scientists continue to live and work at research stations across Antarctica. Most live there only in the summer, but about 1,000 people remain throughout the Antarctic winter. At the South Pole itself, where the Norwegian flag once flapped above a small tent, the large, modern-looking Amundsen–Scott South Pole Station now stands. In place of the dogs that so faithfully pulled the explorers to the South Pole, snowmobiles and airplanes are now the regular modes of transportation. Despite such changes, for the most part, Antarctica still remains the remote, desolate land that Amundsen and his men first marched across—a land that gives the impression, as Amundsen wrote, that "Nature [is] too powerful for us."

All traffic en route to or from the Amundsen–Scott South Pole Station is directed through McMurdo Station, the largest community in Antarctica.

TIMELINE

1872   Roald Amundsen is born on July 16, near Oslo, Norway.

1887   Amundsen decides to become an Arctic explorer after reading about the exploits of Sir John Franklin.

1895   The sixth International Geographical Congress meets in London in July to spur on Antarctic exploration.

1894   Amundsen joins the crew of the sealer *Magdalena*, sailing aboard the ship until 1896.

1897   On August 16, Amundsen sets sail for Antarctica aboard the *Belgica*, which becomes frozen in pack ice in March 1898.

1899   In February, the *Belgica* finally sails free, after the crew blasts a channel through a section of pack ice.

1902   On December 30, Robert Falcon Scott turns back after reaching 82°16′ S on the first-ever expedition to attempt the South Pole.

1903   On June 17, Amundsen sets sail on the *Gjøa*, which he navigates through the Northwest Passage.

1907   On August 7, Ernest Shackleton leaves Britain on an expedition to the South Pole, reaching 88°23′ S in 1909.

1909   Americans Frederick Cook and Robert Peary both claim to have reached the North Pole.

1910   On June 7, the *Fram* leaves Norway for a month-long tour of the North Atlantic.

1910   On August 9, Amundsen sets sail on the *Fram* with 18 men, reportedly heading to the North Pole.

1910   On September 9, in Madeira, Amundsen announces to the crew that the *Fram* is sailing for Antarctica.

1911   The *Fram* crosses the Antarctic Circle on January 2 and on January 14 arrives at the Ross Ice Shelf.

1911   On January 28, Amundsen and eight men move into their winter hut on the Ross Ice Shelf.

1911   From February to April, Amundsen and his men establish supply caches at latitudes 80°, 81°, and 82° S.

1911   Amundsen departs Framheim for the pole on September 8 but is forced to return because of bad weather.

1911   Amundsen and four of the men set out for the South Pole on October 19.

1911   On November 17, Amundsen and his men reach the end of the Ross Ice Shelf.

1911   Amundsen and his party arrive at the true South Pole on December 16.

1912   On January 25, Amundsen and his party return to Framheim.

1912   The *Fram* reaches the Australian island of Tasmania on March 7.

ENDNOTES

AIRSHIP: an aircraft that is lighter than air, has a motor, and can be steered

ANTARCTIC CIRCLE: an imaginary line circling Earth at a latitude of about 66°30′ S, it forms the border of the Antarctic, below which the sun does not set for at least one day in summer and does not rise for at least one day in winter

ARCTIC CIRCLE: an imaginary line circling Earth at a latitude of about 66°30′ N, it forms the border of the Arctic, above which the sun does not set for at least one day in summer and does not rise for at least one day in winter

GLACIER: a large, slow-moving mass of ice and snow that forms in mountains and in regions where more snow falls than can melt each year

HYPSOMETERS: instruments used to measure height above sea level by determining the boiling point of water at a specific location

ICE BELT: a long strip or band of large, floating chunks of ice located in the sea near the solid pack ice

ICE SHELF: a floating, thick mass of ice that is attached to a landmass and is usually landlocked on three sides

LATITUDE: imaginary lines that circle Earth and indicate position north or south of the equator; latitude is measured in degrees, and each line of latitude is divided into 60 minutes (′), which are further divided into 60 seconds (″)

MAGNETIC FIELD: the area around a magnetic object in which the magnet is able to exert a force

NORTHWEST PASSAGE: a water route from the Atlantic Ocean to the Pacific along the northern coast of the North American continent

PACK ICE: sea ice that is afloat and has formed into a large, nearly solid mass

SCURVY: a disease caused by a lack of vitamin C and characterized by weakness and bleeding under the skin

SEXTANTS: instruments used to determine one's position by measuring the height of the sun or stars above the horizon

TREATY: a formal agreement between two or more countries or groups of people

SELECTED BIBLIOGRAPHY

Amundsen, Roald. *My Life as an Explorer*. Garden City, N.Y.: Doubleday, Page & Company, 1927.

——. *The South Pole: An Account of the Norwegian Antarctic Expedition in the "Fram," 1910–1912*. Translated by A. G. Chater. New York: Lee Keedick, 1913.

Heacox, Kim. *Antarctica: The Last Continent*. Washington, D.C.: National Geographic Society, 1998.

Huntford, Roland, ed. *The Amundsen Photographs*. New York: Atlantic Monthly Press, 1987.

Huntford, Roland. *The Last Place on Earth*. New York: Atheneum, 1985.

Kelly, Ned, and Martha Holmes. *Antarctica: Life in the Freezer*. VHS. Washington, D.C.: National Geographic Video, 1993.

McGonigal, David, and Lynn Woodworth. *Antarctica and the Arctic: The Complete Encyclopedia*. Willowdale, Ontario: Firefly Books, 2001.

Norsk Polarhistorie. "Person Gallery." Norsk Polarhistorie. Translated by Google. http://www.polarhistorie.no/personer.

FOR FURTHER READING

Alter, Judy. *Extraordinary Explorers and Adventurers*. New York: Children's Press, 2001.

Broderick, Enid. *Roald Amundsen*. Milwaukee: World Almanac Library, 2002.

Friedman, Mel. *Antarctica*. New York: Children's Press, 2009.

Thompson, Gare. *Roald Amundsen and Robert Scott Race to the South Pole*. Washington, D.C.: National Geographic, 2007.